emotional rescue

First published in the UK in 2018
by Studio Press Books,

an imprint of Kings Road Publishing,
part of Bonnier Books UK,
The Plaza, 535 King's Road,
London, SW10 0SZ

www.studiopressbooks.co.uk
www.bonnierbooks.co.uk

Printed Under License ©2018 Emotional Rescue
www.emotional-rescue.com

1 3 5 7 9 10 8 6 4 2

ISBN 978-1-78741-337-5
Printed in Italy

The Wit & Wisdom of
BROTHER

STUDIO
PRESS

Unless it could play Grand Theft Auto, Bro was not interested.

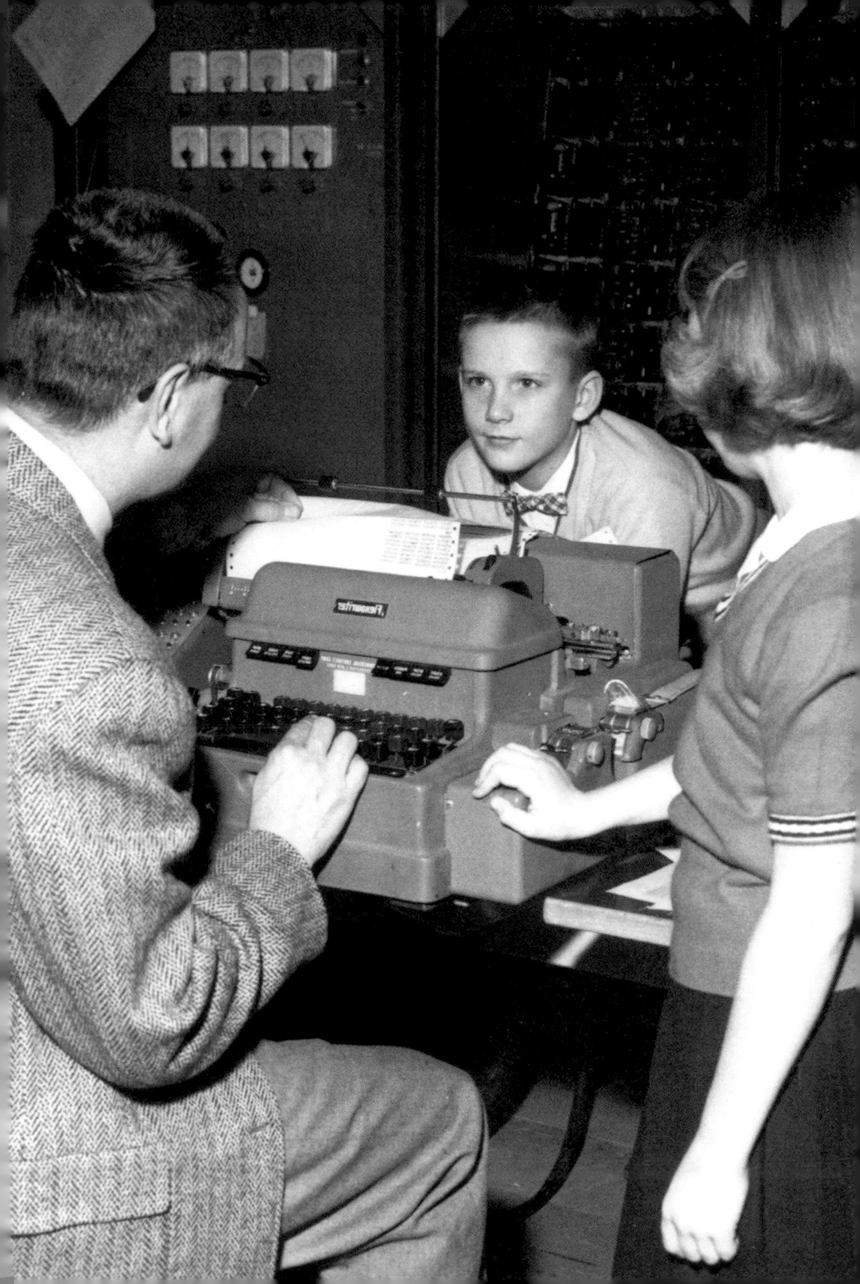

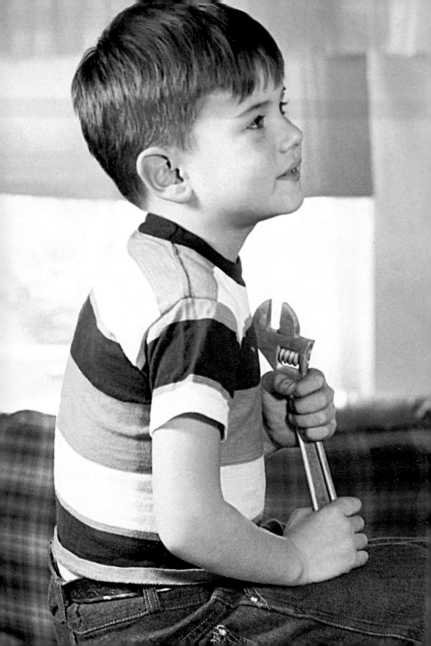

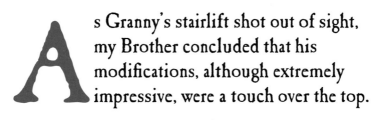

s Granny's stairlift shot out of sight, my Brother concluded that his modifications, although extremely impressive, were a touch over the top.

Whoever said he was 'hard to buy for' must have been as thick as two short planks.

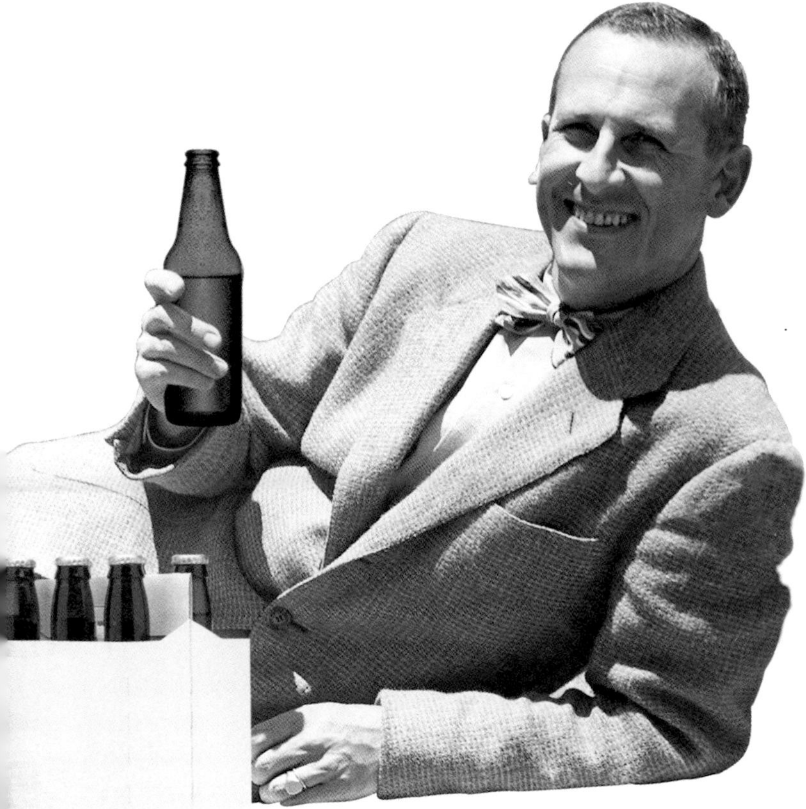

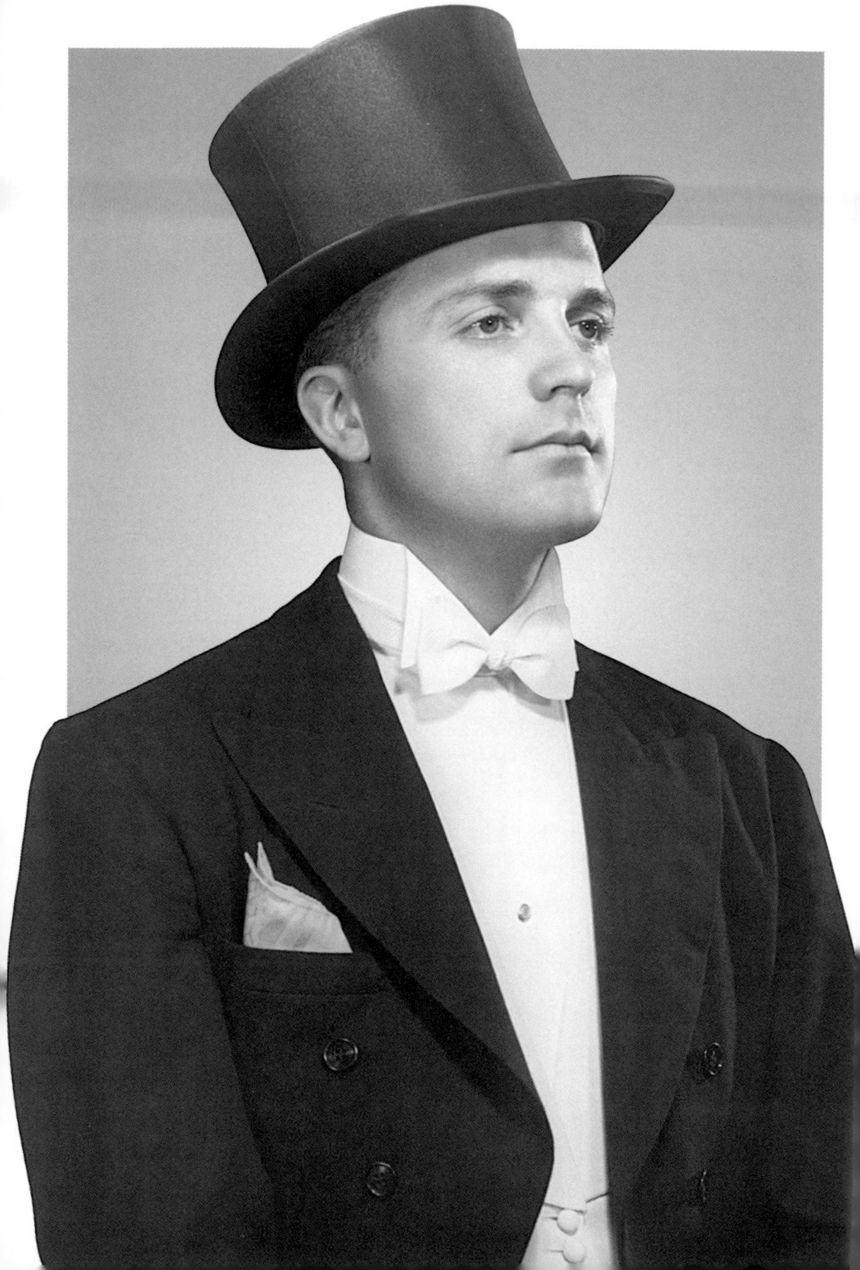

My Brother could often be a bit of a snob – with a silent 's'!

As Bro woke up with a hefty hangover, he just thanked his lucky stars he hadn't done anything embarrassing the night before.

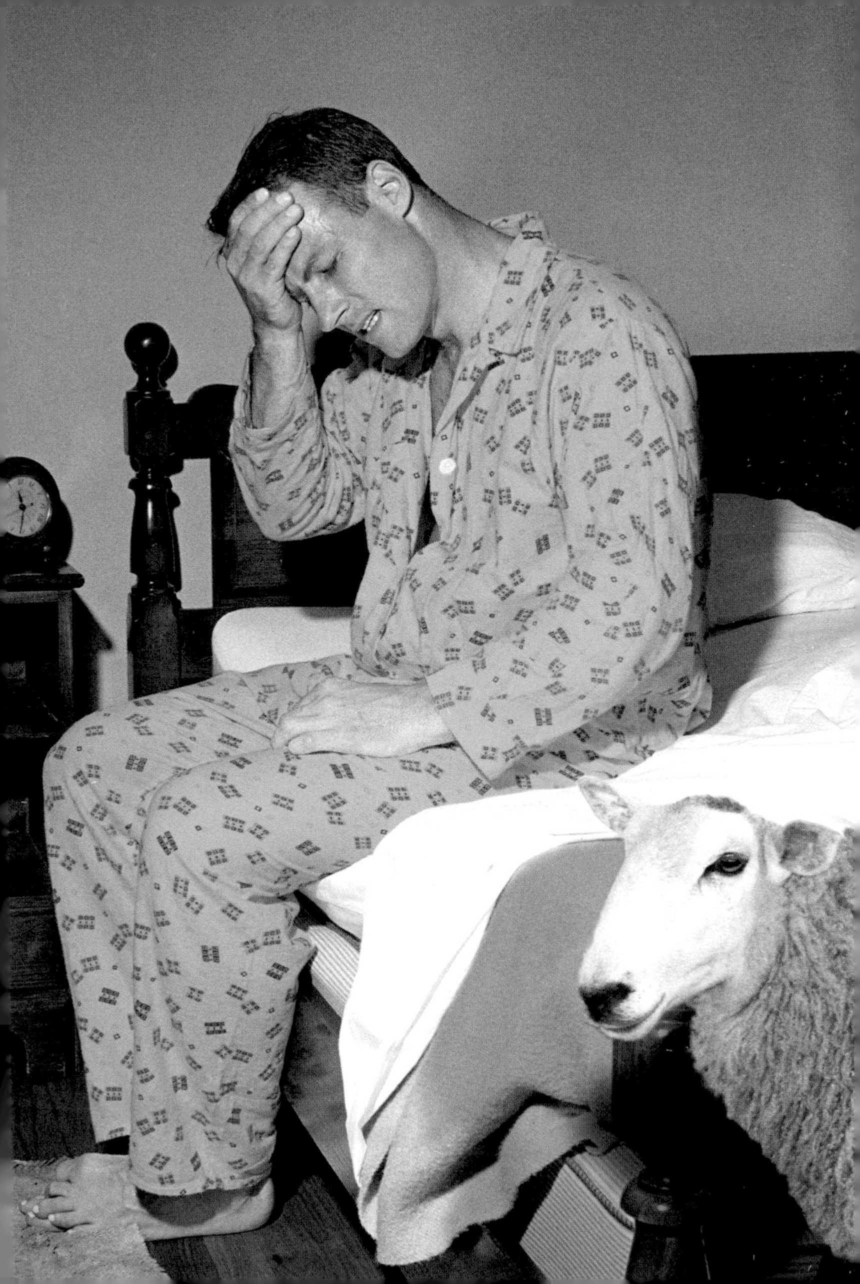

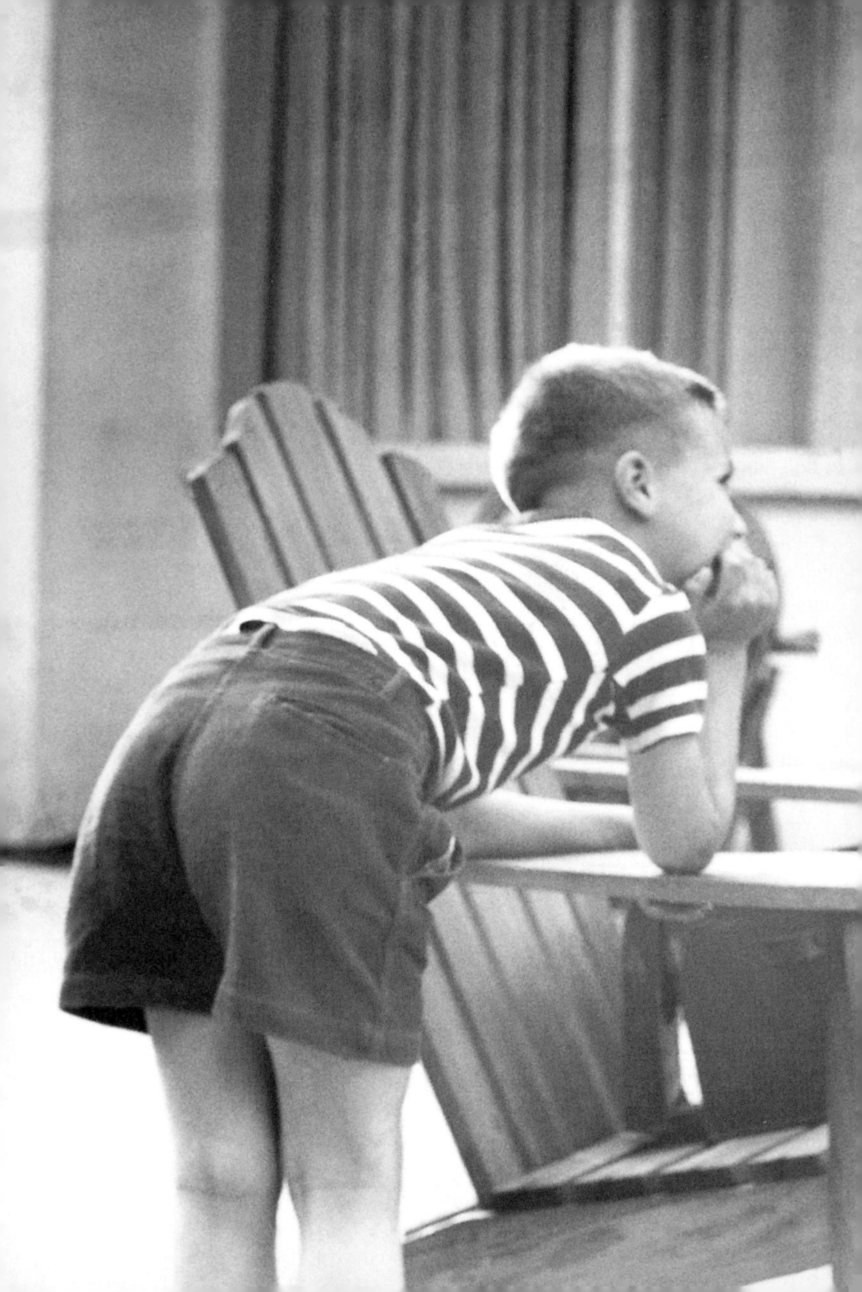

Bro took aim at his family and fired off a couple of rounds from his pump-action bum-gun.

He knew he still had a photographic memory. Unfortunately, it no longer provided same-day delivery.

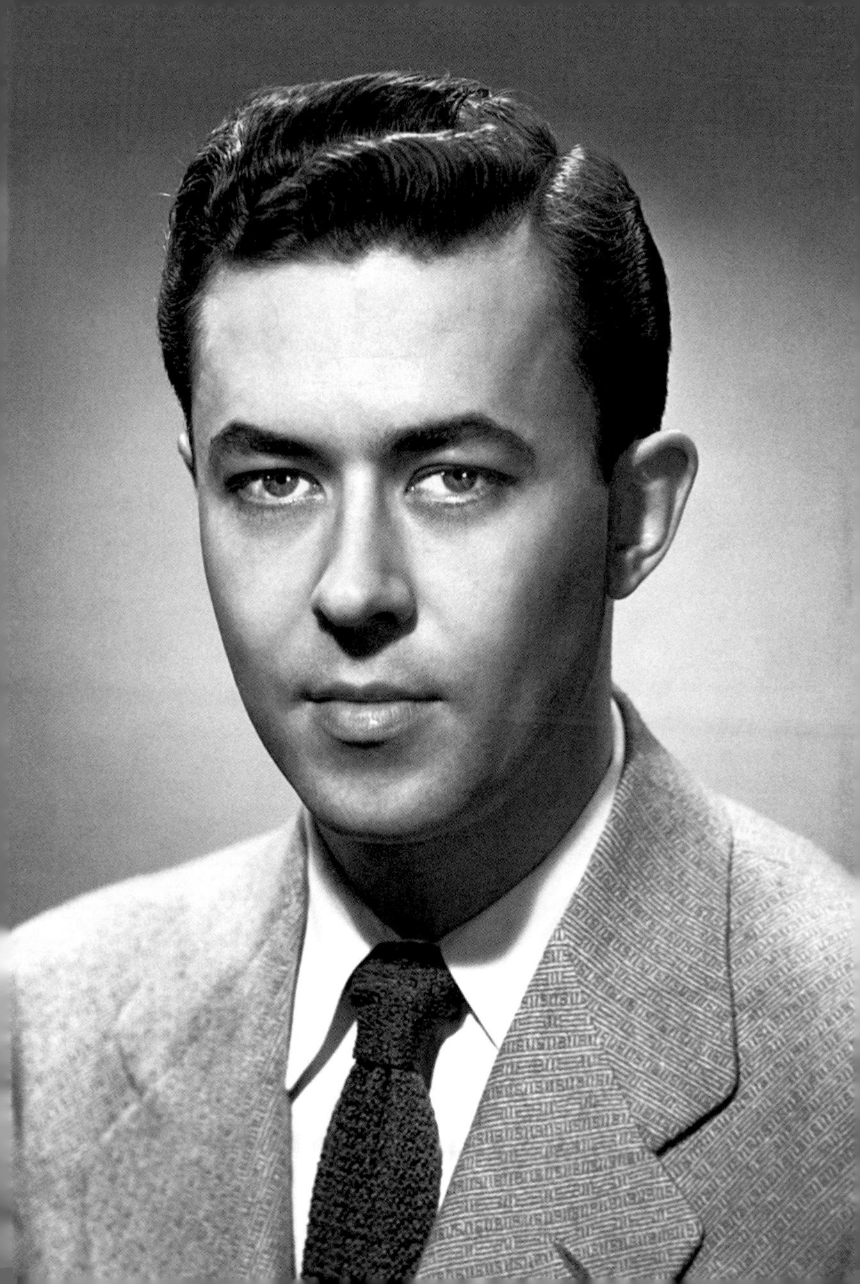

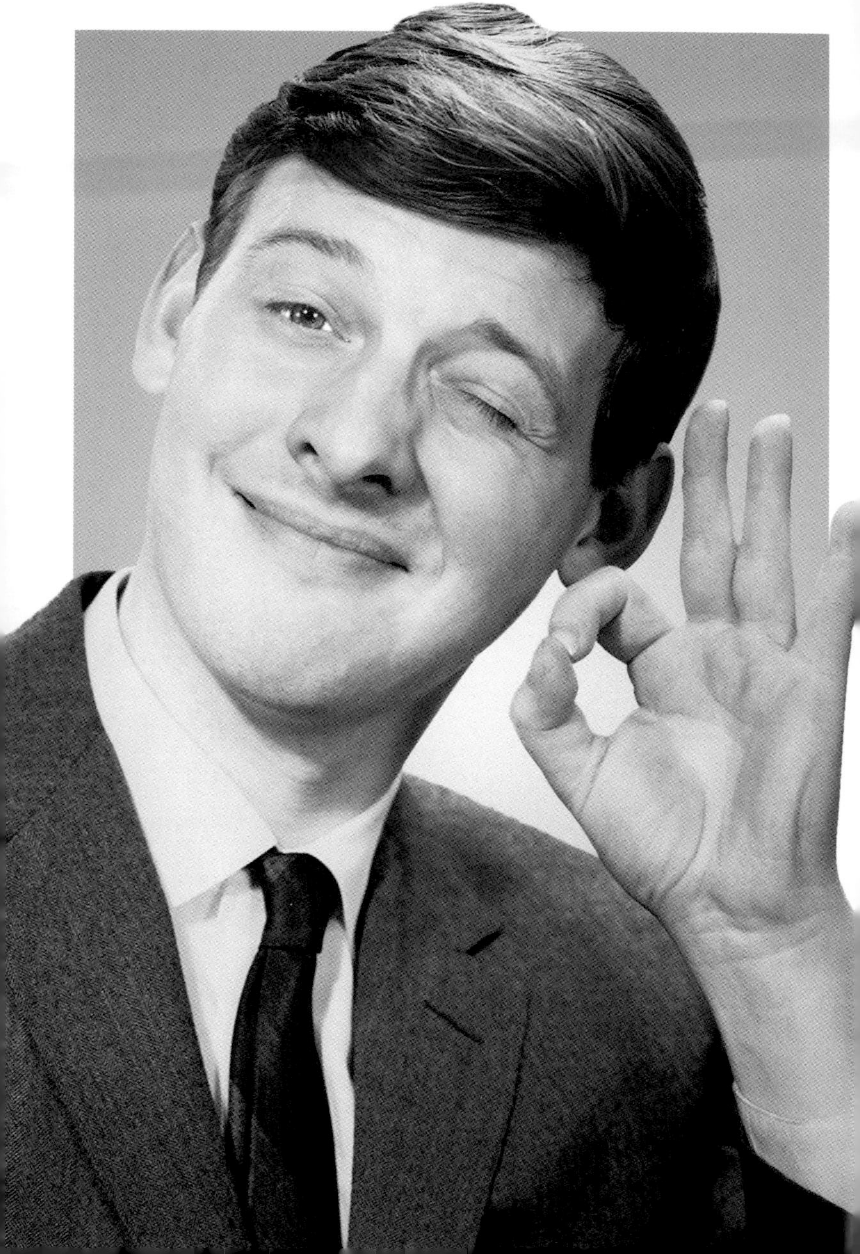

Like most Brothers, he could be a bit of a winker.

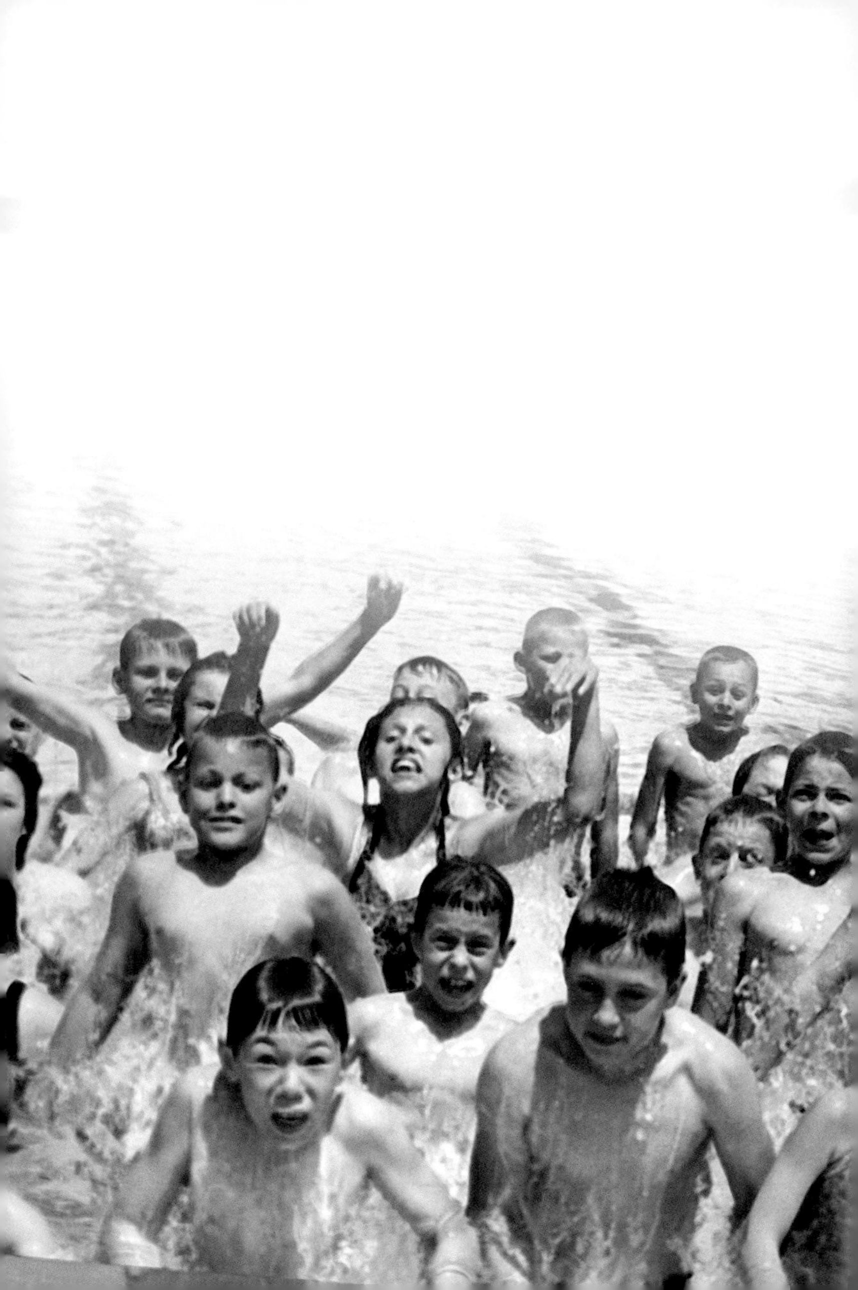

My Brother never expected his floating rubber turd prank would cause so much panic.

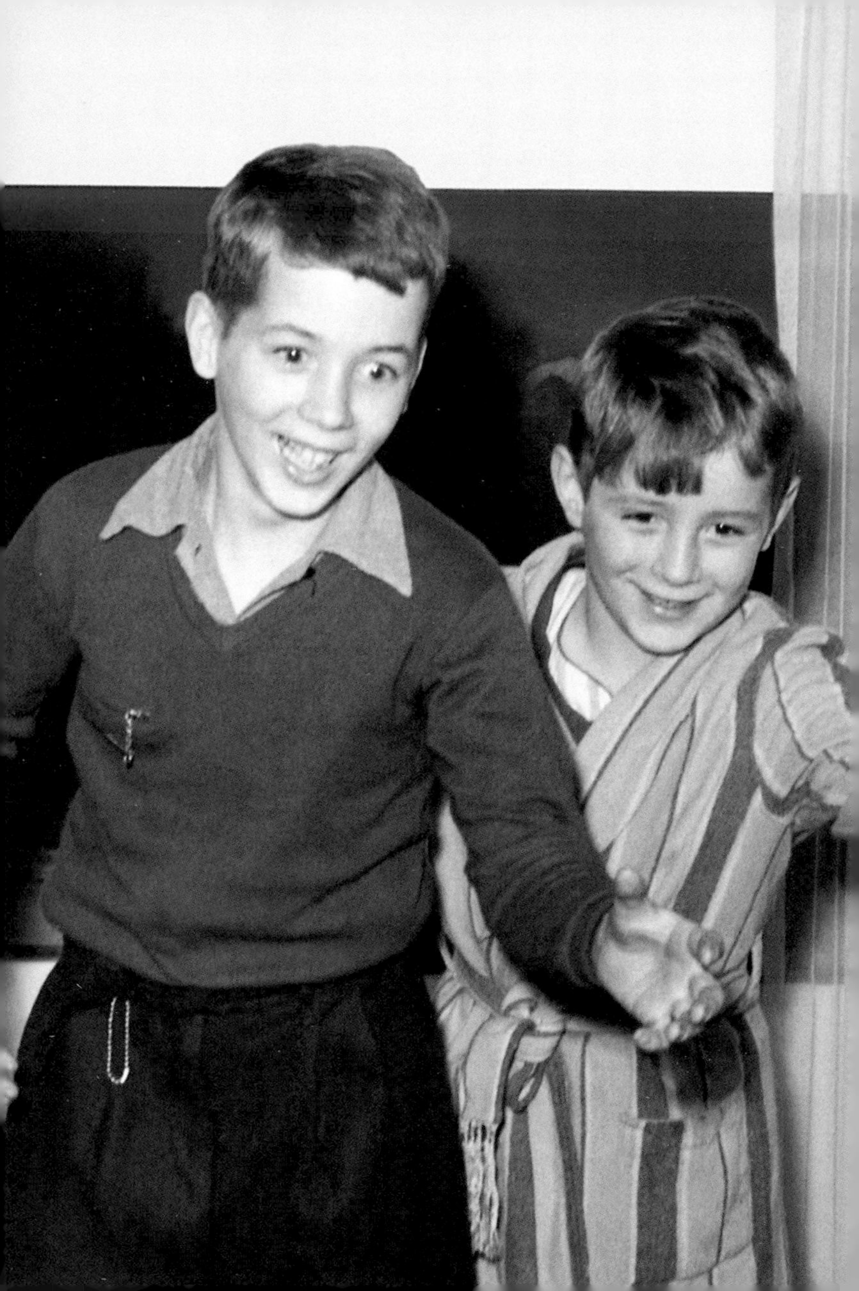

"Look! She's fallen for it again!" laughed the boys as Granny failed to notice that once again they'd loosened all the screws on her zimmer frame.

It was funny as Bro was very much like a bottle of lager... empty from the neck up!

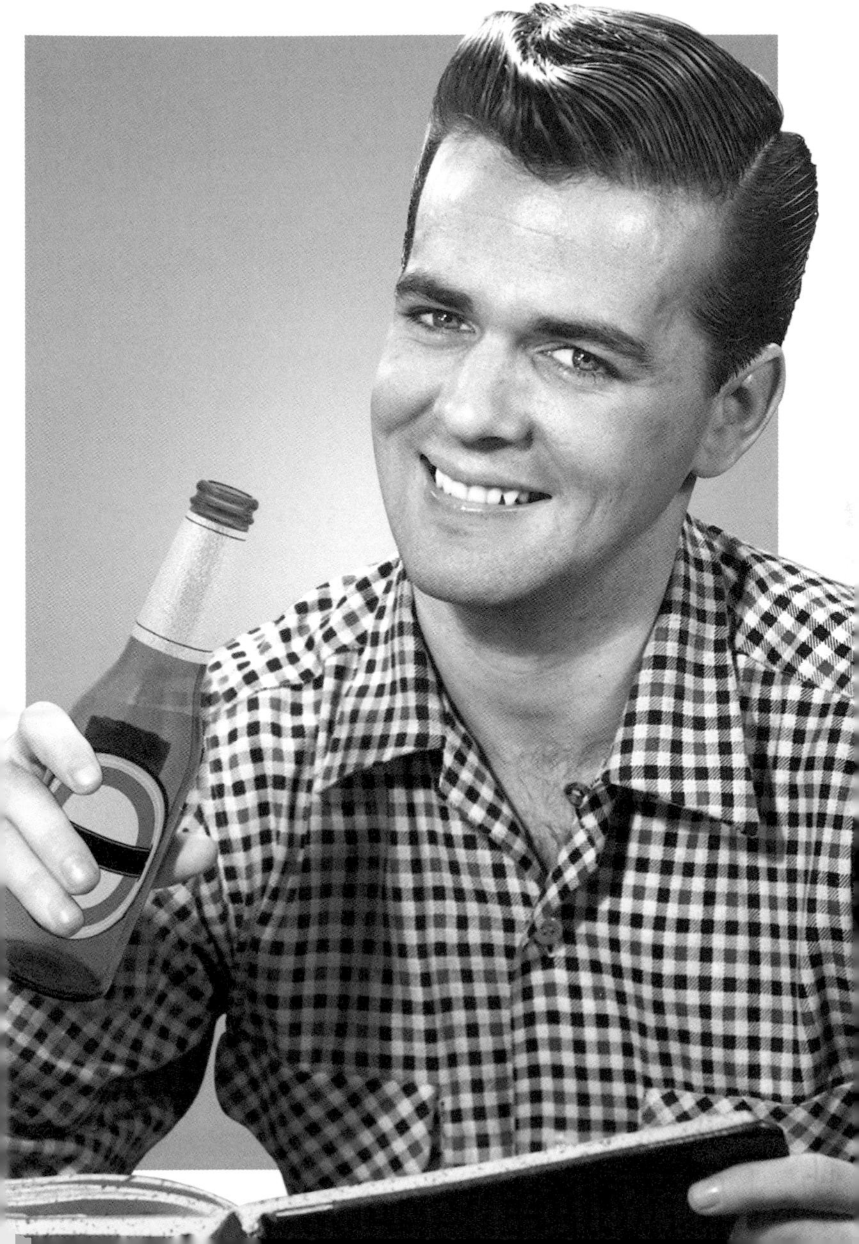

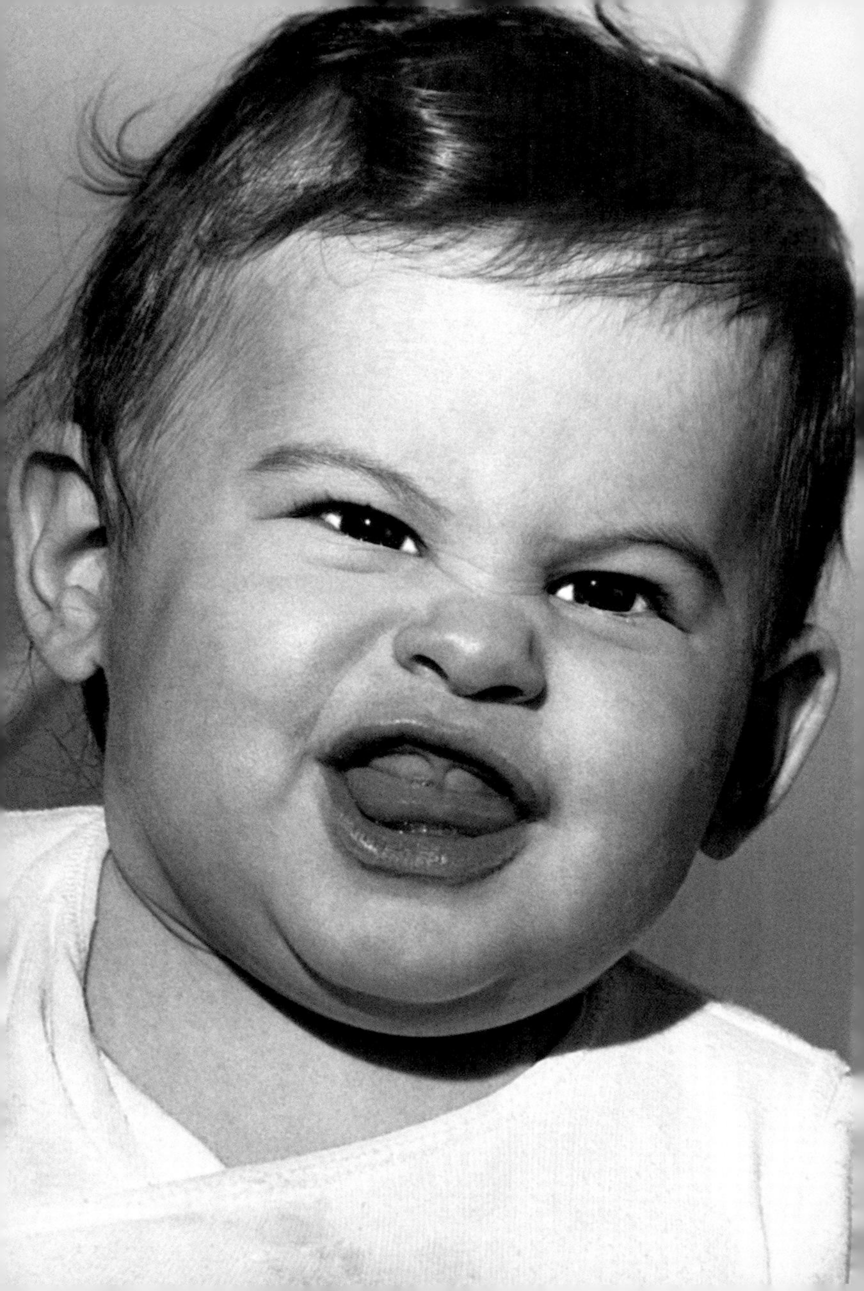

s an infant, Bro discovered that his bot-bot could speak — and that it had very smelly breath!

My brother promised his missus the world. But he still wouldn't give her the remote.

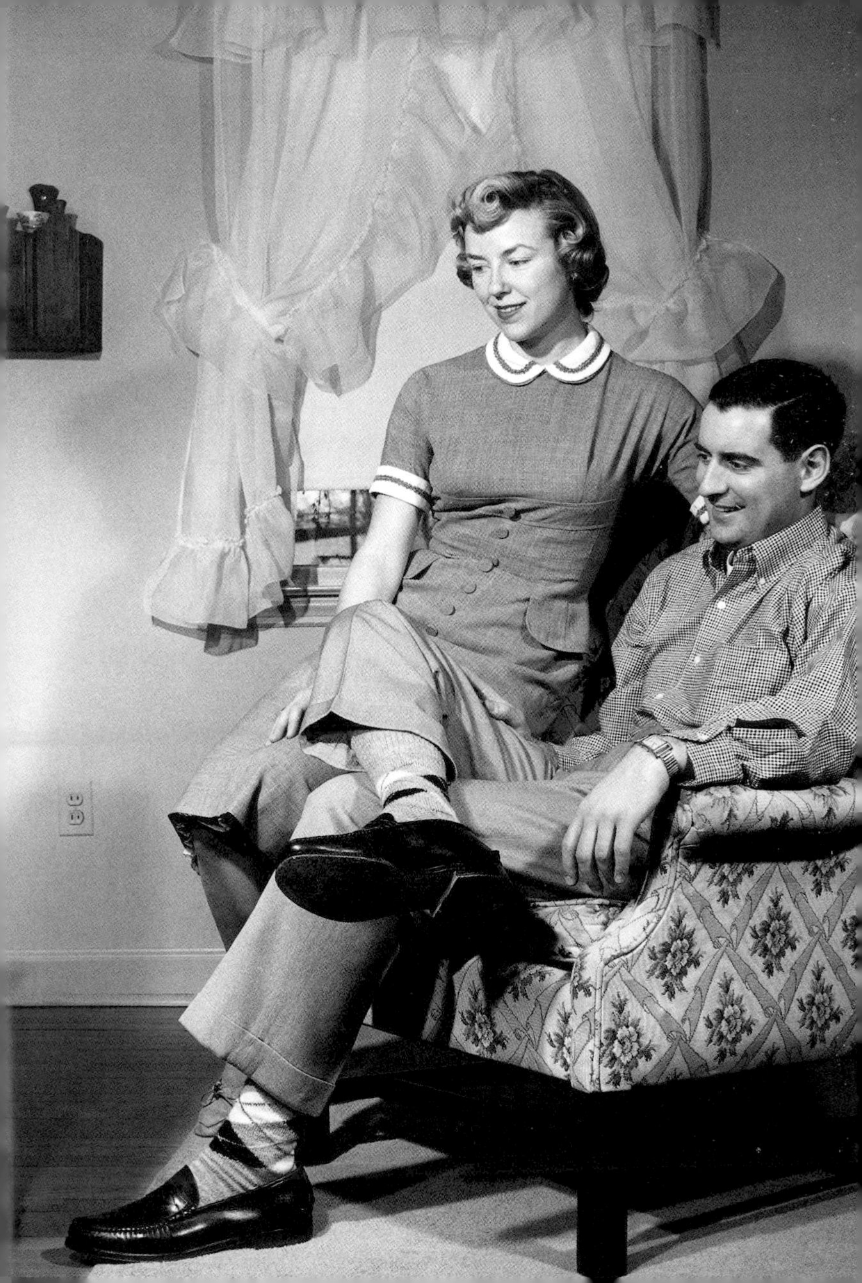

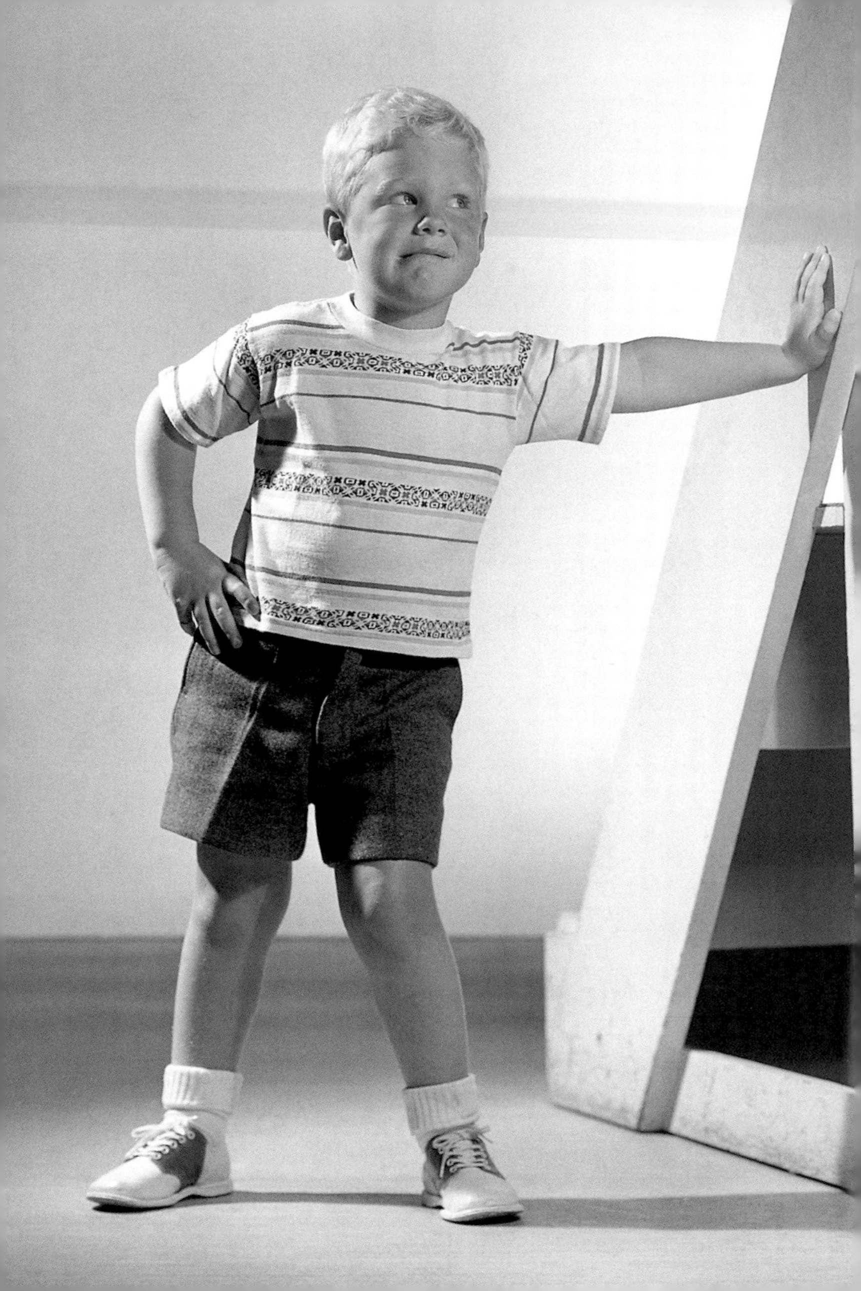

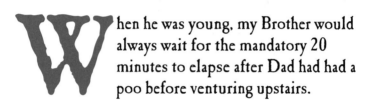

When he was young, my Brother would always wait for the mandatory 20 minutes to elapse after Dad had had a poo before venturing upstairs.

Like a lot of men, he had a habit of fiddling with his nuts.

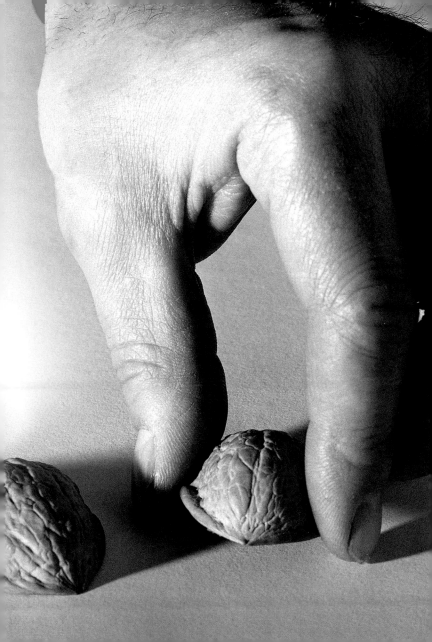

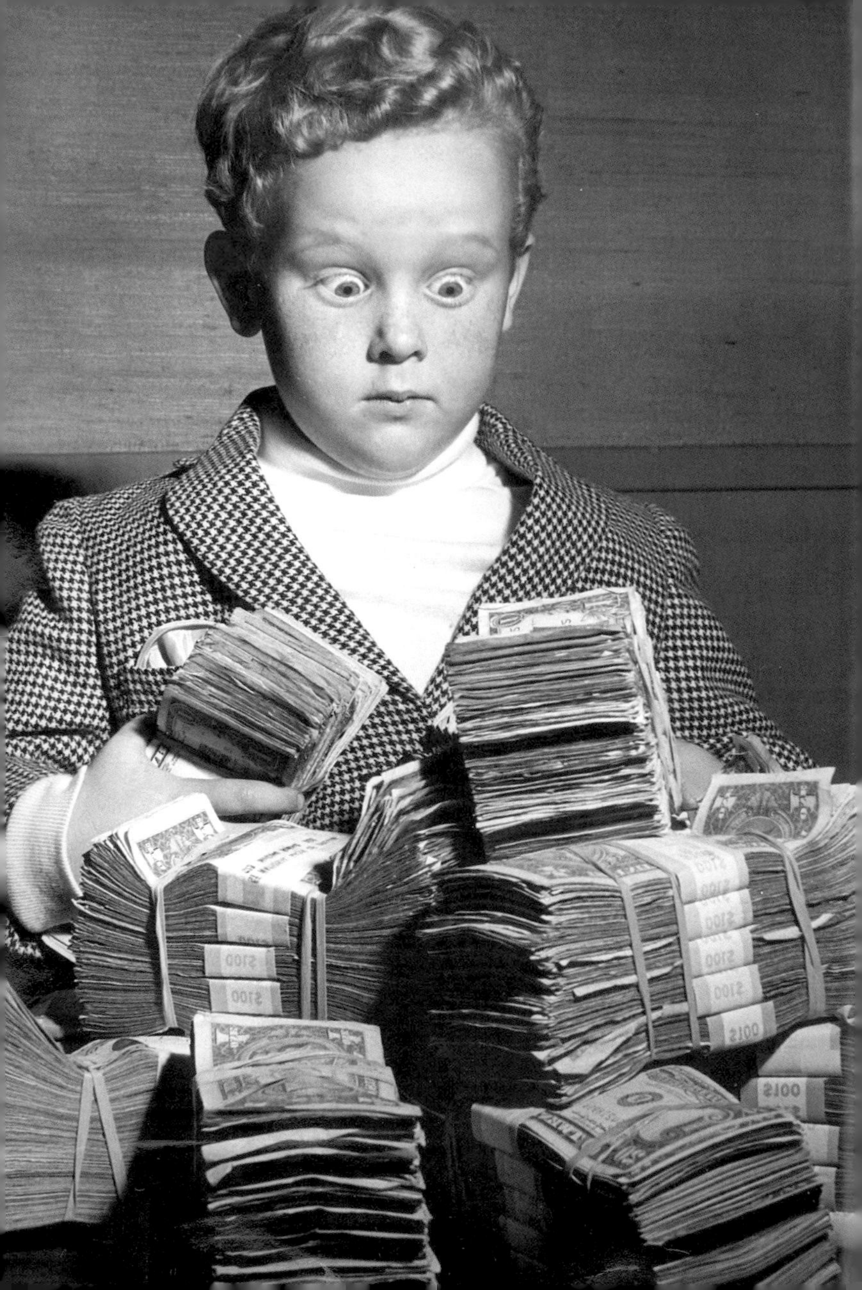
$100

Bro didn't think he'd get this much money selling the family car on eBay!

I t wasn't exactly the Birthday present he had in mind when he said he wanted something from the Apple Store.

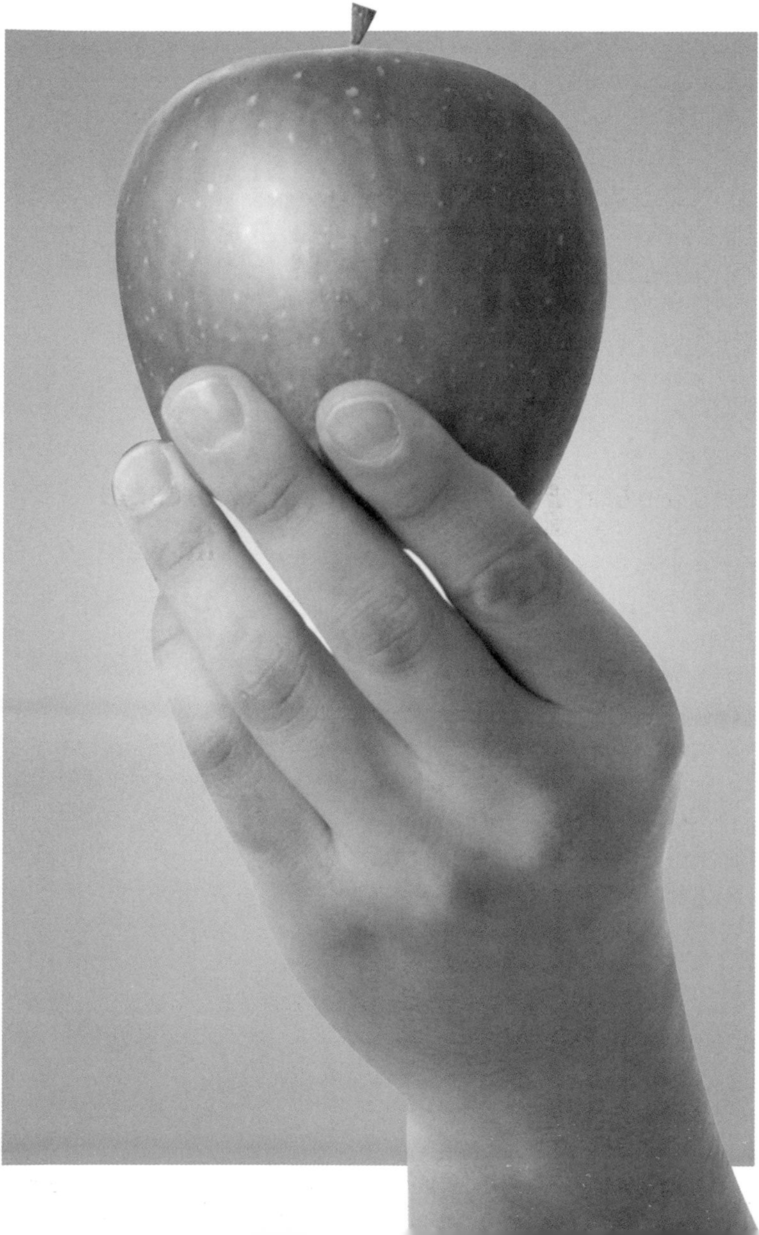

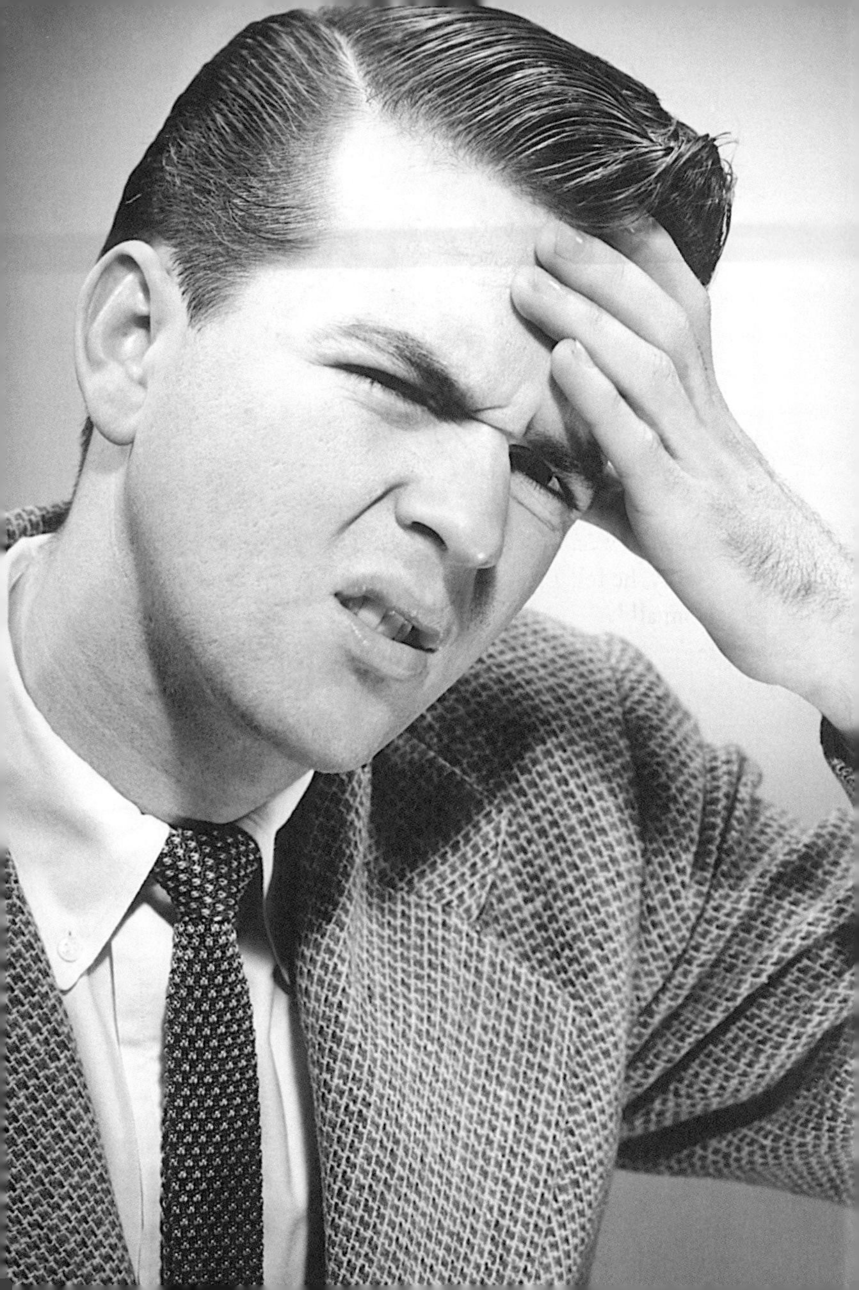

I t was the weekend and he suddenly felt his life was empty, he felt alone, with a sense that he was isolated from all he knew and loved, unable to express his innermost feelings, to share his thoughts, his needs, his...

no wait, wifi seemed to be up and working again now.

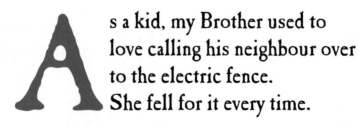

As a kid, my Brother used to love calling his neighbour over to the electric fence.
She fell for it every time.

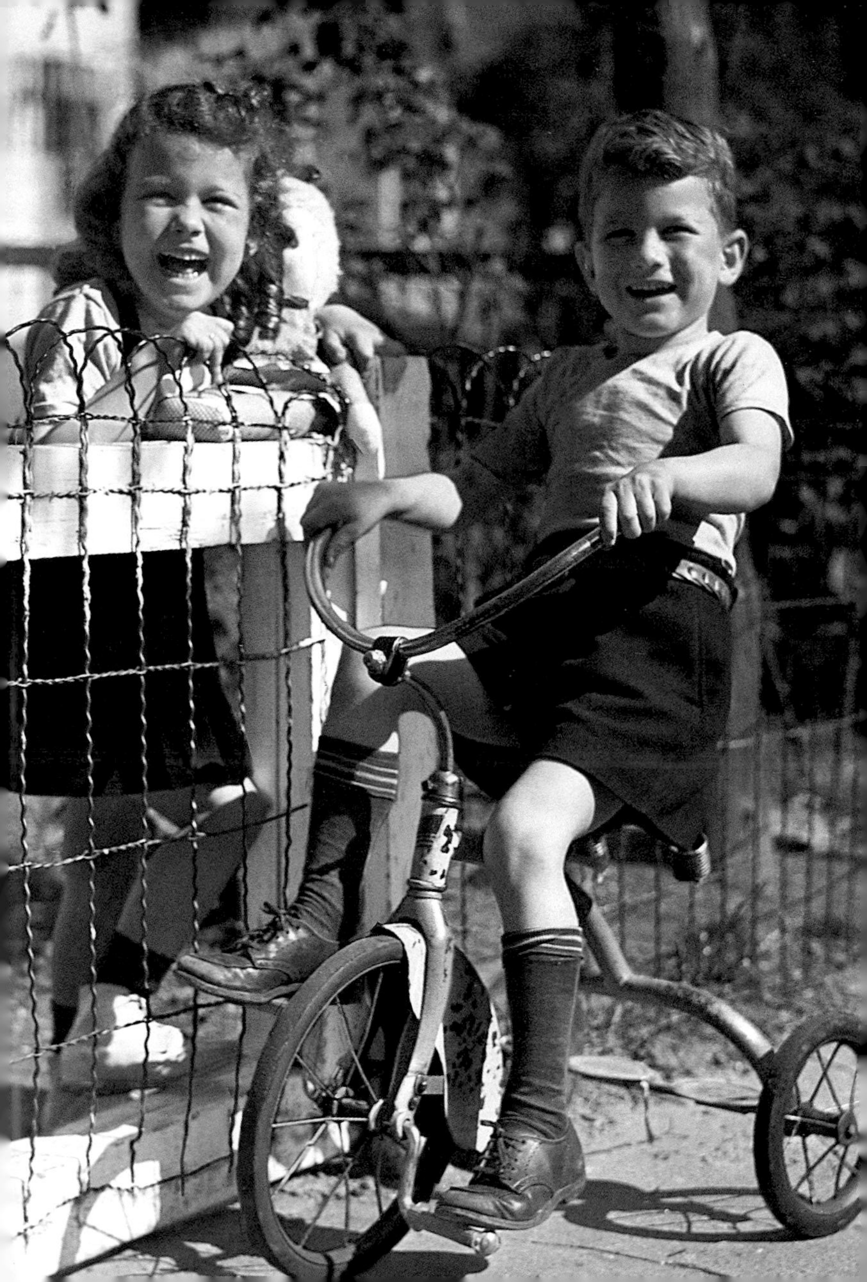

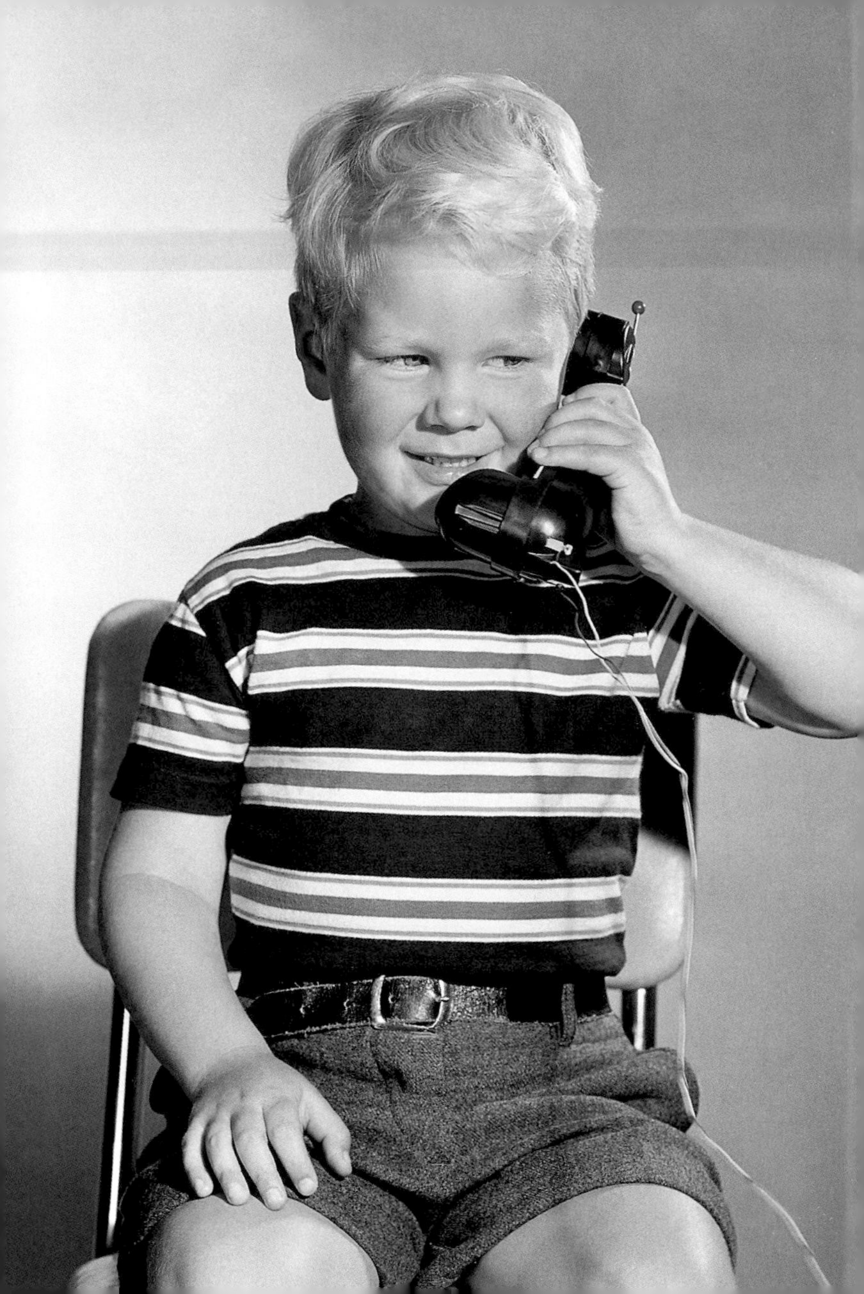

When his Mum screeched that he treated the house like a hotel, my Brother called reception to complain about the maid's attitude.

As another year passed, he reflected on the years of desperation, the almost unimaginable loneliness and the heart-felt yearning for something better... Still, maybe that was the price you paid for supporting a sh*te football club.

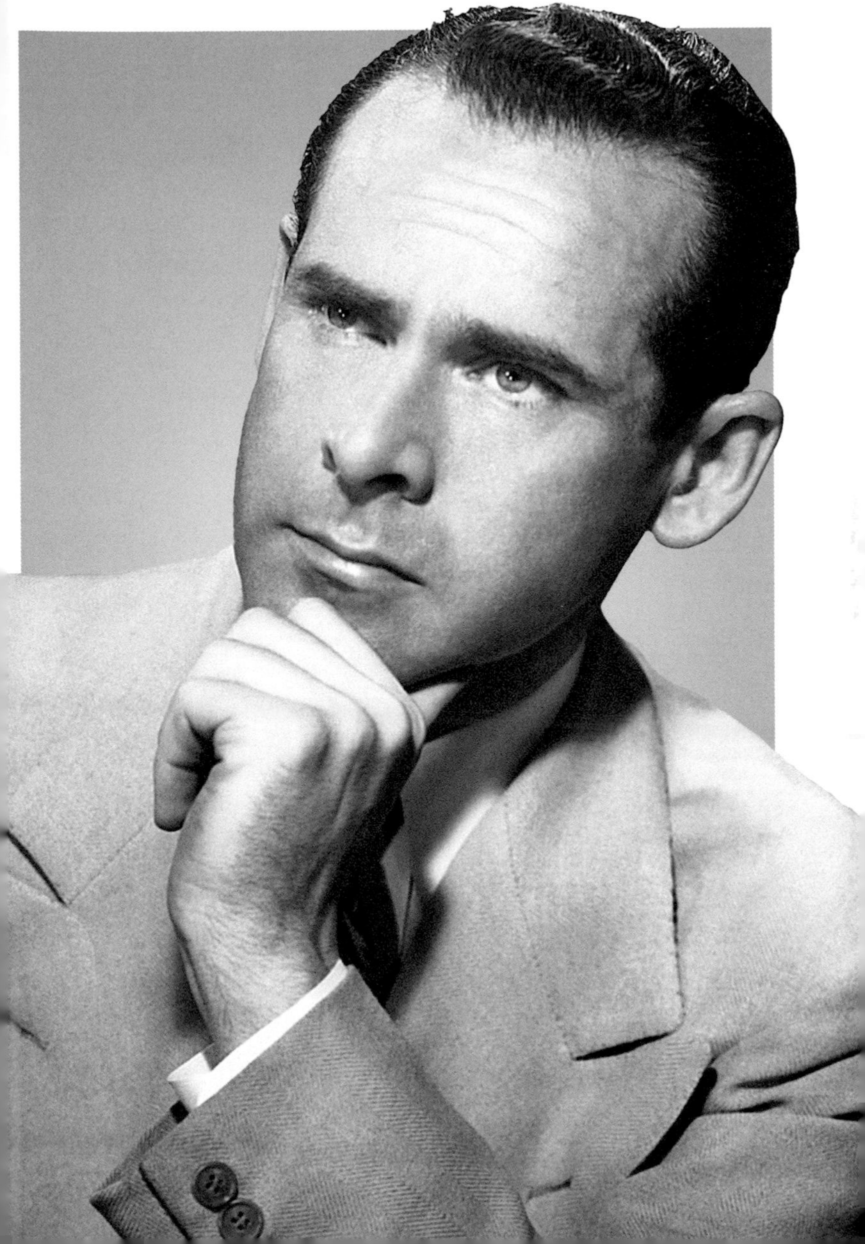

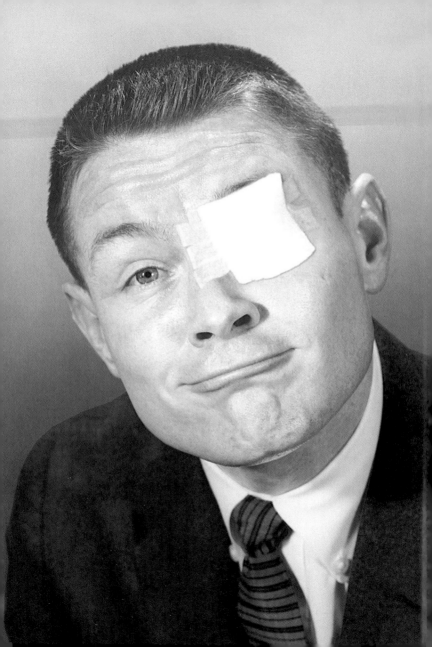

Poor Bro's failure to grasp modern technology was confirmed when he returned from the car boot proudly displaying his new iPad.

Like all little boys he was very grateful in later life for the social skills he'd learned from watching his Dad.

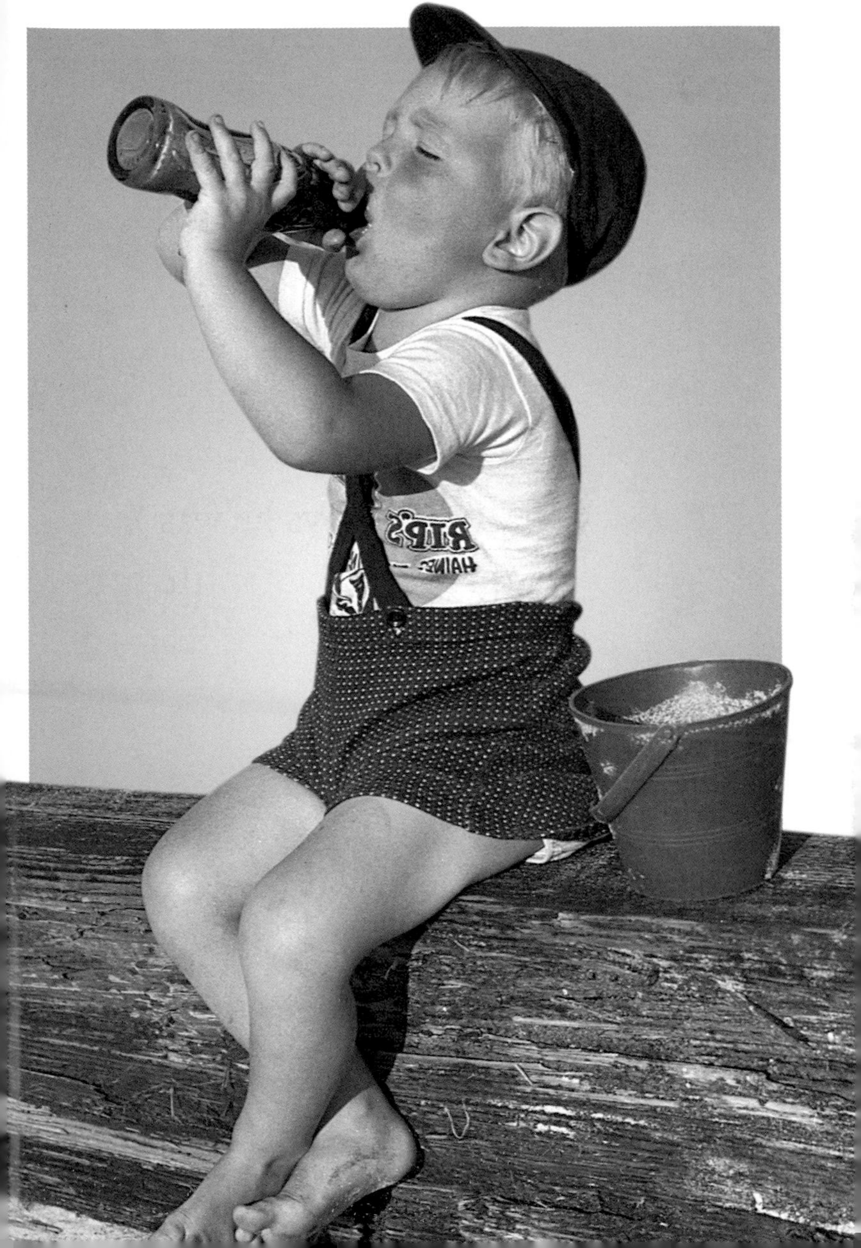

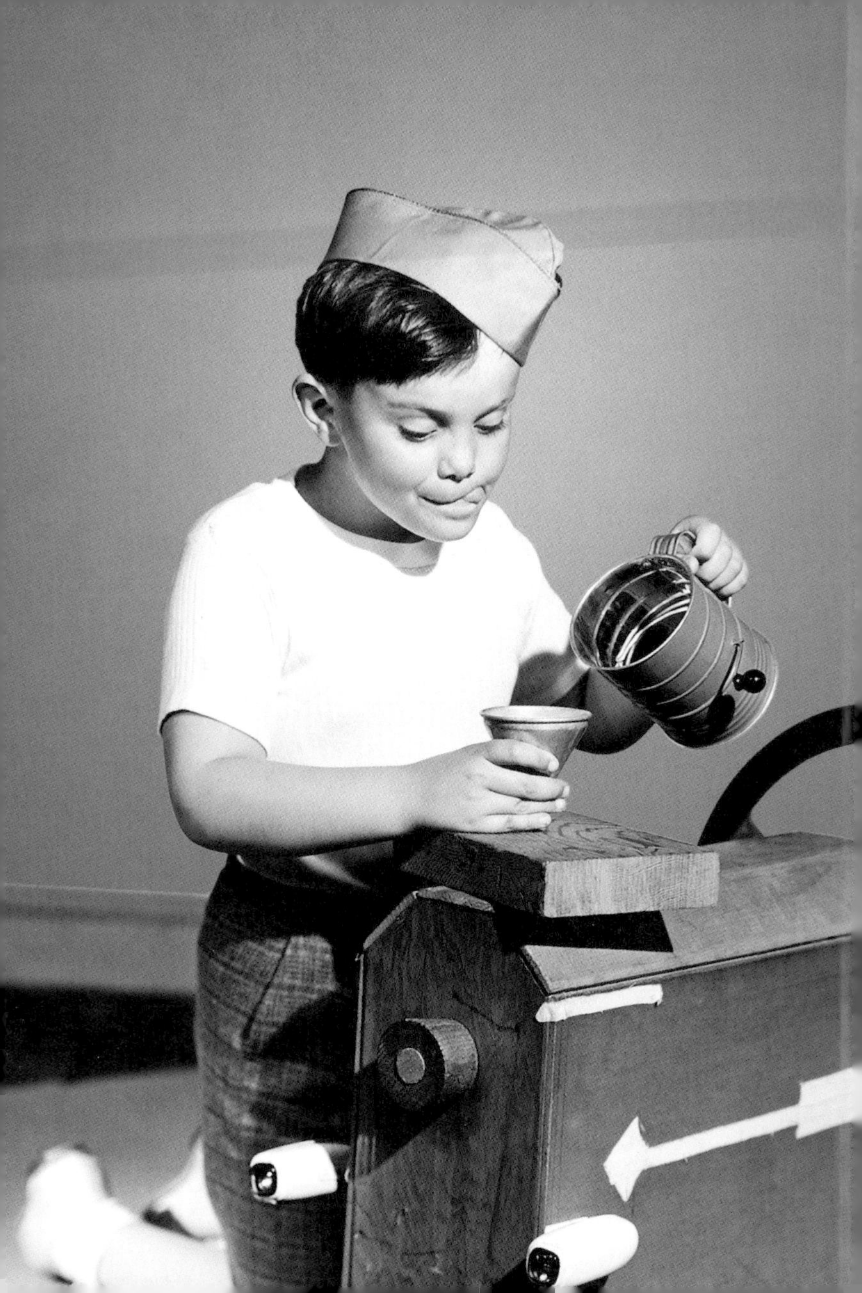

As a child my Brother learned loads of things from watching his Dad do D.I.Y. Mainly, words beginning with F and B.